The Natural Way of Married Life

JOY
IN
HUMAN
SEXUALITY

The Natural Way of Married Life

John T. Ball

and

Nancy Cashman Ball

THE LITURGICAL PRESS
Collegeville, Minnesota

To all who seek to strengthen and renew marriage today, and especially to the many couples in Connecticut who have shared their lives and their love with us during the past nine exciting, fruitful years.

To our two daughters: vivacious Cathy and bright, shining Claire, who constantly remind us of their person-hood and help to deepen in us with each passing year an awareness of the preciousness and the responsibility of the gift of life.

Preface

Two distinct objectives have motivated us to write about the meaning of natural family planning. First, this task has given us the opportunity to critically examine and clarify ideas that have been proposed and developed by many couples over the past nine years. Second, we feel that a very real need exists for expressing these thoughts and experiences in the written word. In recent years several very fine books on the *technique* of natural family planning have been published; however, much less has been written about the *meaning* of natural family planning within the marital relationship. This has created a serious void, especially considering the increased interest in natural family planning in the past few years.

A number of persons have contributed to shaping the text into its final form. We are especially indebted to Mrs. Virginia Gager, whose review, comments, and editorial suggestions were invaluable. Others who provided helpful comments include Rev. Paul Marx, O.S.B., Mr. John G. Quesnell, A.C.S.W., and Mr. William Wholean. We are grateful to each of the above and to all who helped to make this booklet possible.

J.T.B.
N.C.B.

Table of Contents

Introduction

Natural family planning is a way of married life whose time has come. This is, perhaps, a pretentious statement to make, but we intend to show why we feel it is true and what natural family planning can mean for countless married couples in years to come.

What do we mean by "natural family planning"? The first and most obvious meaning is the achievement of an awareness and an understanding of the fertile and infertile phases of a woman's menstrual cycle. With this knowledge, a married couple can regulate the conception of new life. The ability to recognize the time of fertility has increased markedly during the past fifteen years, both from improved application of existing knowledge of the cycle and from further developments in such knowledge. There is no longer any doubt that the means exist for reliably monitoring the fertile and infertile phases of the menstrual cycle; they have been well documented in several recent books, which we list in the bibliography and will cite in appropriate chapters.

Now a more basic question must be asked: Why bother with natural family planning? Why take the trouble, when there are so many "convenient" contraceptive methods? Although the answers to these questions are not immediately obvious, this does not mean that they are unimportant or unrelated to everyday living in marriage and family life.

Modern man, with his enormously fruitful advances in science and technology, has carved out a world of specialties and specialists. The scientific method and the logical approach to investigating a problem have provided technological marvels. At the same time, they have produced a marked tendency to isolate a problem, develop a technique for solving it, and then apply the technique—period! Some obvious difficulties arise from this approach, even when we consider only the physical environment. Rapid, unquestioning applications of technology have often produced secondary and tertiary effects, both foreseen and unforeseen, which have created the crisis of air, water, and noise pollution that commands so much attention today. We now realize that the natural environment must be considered as a whole and that a myriad of complex and subtle interrelationships can upset the ecological balance.

There is a lesson to be learned here when we consider human relationships and the environment of marriage and the family. Too often in the past, the question of family planning was viewed narrowly as an isolated problem which could be "dealt with" without reflecting any further than whether a given technique worked (i.e., it prevented conception). Indeed, the prevention of conception becomes the ultimate good in a society which is dedicated to zero or negative population growth as a means of attaining ever higher levels of affluence and consumption. The fruits of such a mentality become increasingly apparent as time passes—boredom, lack of trust, lack of purpose or commitment. Legalized abortion-on-demand seems to be only the beginning of a general erosion of the value in which human life has traditionally been held. People who find their own lives of little value and who vainly try to ward off despair can hardly be expected to cherish uterine life.

In reality, a married couple's approach to family planning profoundly affects their relationship with each other and their philosophy of life. Many of the effects may be unperceived, but they are nonetheless very real. The meaning of conjugal love and an understanding of personhood and of human sexuality cannot be separated from the fully human power of generating new life. A technical solution to family planning which eliminates this power, i.e., contraception, is much more than a "triumph" of man over the "consequences" of his biology—it is a statement of how he views himself. What at first glance seems to produce the freedom of separating coital sexual intercourse from its procreative potential proves ultimately to produce yet another dependency on technology. Physical apparatus or chemicals or a combination of these ushers in a new age of human bondage.

The approach of natural family planning is fundamentally different. It both recognizes and values the procreative and the unitive dimensions of coital sexual intercourse as a dual reality. Rather than eliminating their fertility, a couple live in awareness of it. They do not regard the fully human power to generate new life as opposed to conjugal love. A couple accept the challenge of exercising their stewardship of this power *within* the dynamics of their conjugal relationship.

The full meaning of responsible regulation of conception is apparent only when one squarely faces the question of periodic continence in relationship to human sexuality and conjugal love. Periodic continence refers to the couple's decision to express their love through coital sexual intercourse only during the infertile time, out of respect for their procreative fertility, if they have decided to avoid conception of new life. The creative possibilities of periodic continence can be realized only when the full meaning of conjugal love is perceived by both husband and wife.

Deepening the meaning of conjugal love and broadening our understanding of human sexuality in our society is an enormous task. Far too often, expressing one's sexuality is equated with coital sexual intercourse, and it is then that a couple are said to be "making love." The words we use are very important clues to meanings that we attach to our actions. How absurd to think that love can be made or turned on and off, as if we were conjugal machines! Love begins, first of all, with the total acceptance and giving of oneself, and the total acceptance and receiving of another. Lovingly expressing our sexual selves to husband or wife occurs in all actions in our marriage. Coital sexual intercourse is a unique way of expressing love in marriage, but it is only one of many ways.

When a couple reach the decision to regulate procreation of new life through periodic continence, they continue to express their sexuality and love during the fertile time of the menstrual cycle. This gets to the heart of the matter of understanding the value of natural family planning. It also is the core of most objections to this way of married life. Does the practice of periodic continence offer a means for a couple to deepen their love for each other and achieve greater maturity? Or does it impose an artificial, harmful restraint on a couple? We deeply believe in the positive value of natural family planning. This belief comes from our ten years of married life and from the experiences of countless couples who have shared with us some of the deepest meanings of their marriages.

The translation of these experiences and impressions into words is often a difficult process. However, we have been aided by a number of fine books dealing with love, marriage, and human sexuality. We have been particularly influenced by our friends Robert and Mary Joyce, who have developed revolutionary concepts of human sexuality and marriage in a series of books published during the past five years. In subsequent chapters we will develop and add to the ideas expressed in this introduction. Since our perspective and understanding are closely related to experiences of the past ten years, we will describe some of these experiences, together with our resultant evolution of thought.

1

A Personal Odyssey:
Couple-to-Couple

Over nine years ago, on a balmy September evening, we drove from Hartford to New Haven, Connecticut, in search of a solution to a problem. Nine years is a long time in today's fast-moving age. The space program was still novel, abortion (at least among Catholics) was a closed issue, and the bitter public debate in the Church over contraception was only starting to heat up.

After a year of marriage and our first child, we started to reflect seriously on the meaning of perhaps thirty more years of fertility. We were concerned with planning our family, using the best available natural "method." That September evening in 1965, we did indeed find a method—the Sympto-Thermic Method of family planning. More importantly, though, we embarked upon a course of events that has fundamentally affected and enriched our lives and our marriage.

In a crowded lecture hall, the newly formed Natural Family Planning Association (NFPA) of Connecticut held its first public meeting to present information on the Sympto-Thermic Method and to offer counseling by a trained NFPA couple to those who wished to plan their family. Couples were also encouraged to participate actively in the teaching program of the association by entering a six-session training course. Intrigued with the couple-to-couple concept, we signed up for the training course and, without knowing it, began an adventure that is still unfolding.

The couple-to-couple approach is best understood in the light of several discoveries: (1) the regulation of conception is an integral facet of the marriage relationship; (2) reliable means for regulating conception are available; (3) married couples are ideally suited to teach this knowledge.

First, family planning or conception regulation *is* a vital basic element in each marriage, and as such is the joint responsibility of both husband and wife. It is *not* a medical problem requiring the ongoing assistance of a physician, except in rare instances. It cannot be considered an isolated question to be "taken care of" by one partner, since its disposition profoundly affects the total marriage relationship. If a husband and wife can together assume responsibility for this most fundamental decision of procreating new life, they can share other important decisions in marriage.

Second, the Sympto-Thermic and Ovulation Methods do provide the means whereby a couple can be aware of their fertility with sufficient knowledge to regulate conception reliably. Fertility awareness is achieved through the interpretation of certain feminine bodily signs (principally vaginal mucus discharge) associated with and preceding ovulation, and through the observation of a rise in the basal body temperature and a change in mucus following ovulation. The mucus changes and their relation to fertility have been described by Dr. John J. Billings.[1] The combined use of basal body temperature readings with mucus interpretations is discussed by Paul Thyma.[2] A number of other references outlining the basis for natural family planning are cited in the bibliography.

The reliability of basal body temperature has been attested to by so noted an authority as Dr. Christopher Tietze of the World Population Council. In 1970, at a meeting of the American Association of Planned Parenthood Physicians in Boston, he stated:

> In the present paper, contraceptive methods currently in use are ranked from A to D in descending order, according to their estimated theoretical effectiveness. The four categories are: Most effective, highly effective, less effective, and least effective. The "*most effective*" *group* covers surgical sterilization, oral contraceptives (OC's) of the combined and sequential types, injectable progestational agents, and *temperature rhythm*"[3] (italics added).

[1] John J. Billings, *Natural Family Planning—The Ovulation Method* (Collegeville, Minn.: The Liturgical Press, 1975), pp. 18–19.

[2] Paul Thyma, *The Double Check Method of Natural Family Planning* (Fall River, Mass.: Married Life Information Service, 1976).

[3] Christopher Tietze, "Ranking of Contraceptive Methods by Levels of Effectiveness" (Boston: American Association of Planned Parenthood Physicians, April 9–10, 1970), p. 1.

The real issue is not reliability but whether one views the temperature-mucus observations as another contraceptive method or as a means toward fertility awareness.

Third, couples who are planning their families in awareness of their fertility are ideally suited, given sufficient training, to help other couples. Married couples relate favorably to other married couples and can give initial support and understanding based on personal experience. The help and encouragement that a teacher-couple provide during the first few months after explaining the Sympto-Thermic Method to another couple can make a vital difference. We have seen numerous couples achieve security and serenity in monitoring their fertility, after expressing hesitance and doubt in an initial teaching session. The interpretation of bodily signs and the shift in basal body temperature can be most quickly learned when another couple are readily available for continuing consultative help, which can usually be given in discussion by telephone. Conversely, the time which might be required during these first few months severely limits the number of couples whom a single busy physician could hope to help. The couple-to-couple approach seems to us to be the only realistic way in which significant numbers of couples can acquire knowledge that fosters fertility awareness.

The couple-to-couple approach has reached many couples. SERENA, the senior couple-to-couple organization in this hemisphere, has taught the Sympto-Thermic Method to over forty thousand Canadian couples since 1955. The couple-to-couple program did not begin in the United States until 1965, with the formation of NFPA of Connecticut and Fertility - Love - Insight - Counsel (FLIC) in New Jersey. Since that time, groups have been formed in many states of the United States, reaching thousands of couples. In 1967 a research study conducted in association with Fairfield University demonstrated both the effectiveness of the Sympto-Thermic Method and the validity of Connecticut's couple-to-couple approach. Within the scope of this chapter we can only mention the very extensive work that has been undertaken with the Sympto-Thermic Method and the couple-teaching approach in France, in other countries of Europe, and in many developing countries.

While couple-to-couple teaching is an exciting and revolutionary approach to understanding the ebb and flow of procreative potential, it is but part of the adventure to which we alluded. Added adventure has come from the search, with other couples active in the Couple-to-Couple Movement, into the meaning of respecting this procreative potential. Family planning can come to mean the conscious knowledge of the procreative potential of each coital expression of love. When a couple, aware of this procreative dimension, call forth God's cooperation, they most fully participate in the procreation of new life. The knowledge provided by the Sympto-Thermic and Ovulation Methods has helped many supposedly infertile couples to conceive.

If husband and wife refrain from coitus during the peak of their procreative potential, they renew their witness to each other of their respect for this potential. However, continence during the fertile time should not stifle their mutual expressions of love. Rather, husband and wife are challenged to increase their "response-ability" to each other and continue to express their love creatively. A couple can especially recognize and foster their creativity when respecting their procreative potential.

The adventure, thus, is one of a continuing exploration of the dynamics of conjugal love. All couples can, and perhaps many do, experience a growth in love and understanding of their commitment during their marriage. It seems to us, however, that this growth is greatly enhanced by an awareness of the insights and experiences which other married couples can share.

For us, there has been an evolution in the meaning of couple-to-couple through the years. At first, perhaps, to support another couple consisted in helping them "get through" the period of continence with words of encouragement that "the sacrifice would contribute to a better marriage." At that point, eight or so years ago, the "use" of the Sympto-Thermic Method was for most couples, including ourselves, a way to plan a family reliably without resorting to contraception. A couple were supported by being helped to establish confidence in the reliability of the method and by encouraging them in the idea that it was possible to practice periodic continence.

However, as ideas and questions were expressed by many couples, we noted that periodic continence touched the marriage relationship at a level other than that of family planning. Many couples who felt that they had a good marriage experienced an intense growth in their caring for, and commitment to, each other. They discovered that they were exploring many ways of expressing their love for each other and of being in love each day.

As a couple's mutual respect and trust deepen, new depths of relationship with other couples become possible. The new intensity of the conjugal relationship generates love which overflows to others. Because of the deeper trust in marital relationships, there is more freedom in a spouse's relationship with other people, without creating strong jealousy patterns.

Naturally respecting fertility seems also to be a natural way for the conjugal love of a couple to deepen. The Couple-to-Couple Movement is *not* dedicated to solving the "problem" of family planning. It *is* dedicated to fostering a way of life that will enrich a couple's conjugal love through a deeper understanding of the meaning of the mystery of their conjugal love and procreative power.

2

Self-knowledge
and Procreation

"Some Pharisees asked Jesus when the kingdom of God would come. His answer was, 'The kingdom of God does not come in such a way as to be seen. No one will say, "Look, here it is," or, "There it is!" because the kingdom of God is within you' " (Luke 17:20-21).

Love of God, love of our spouse, and love of all our brothers and sisters in the human family are more likely to increase if we first accept and love ourselves. But to accept and love ourselves truly, we must first know ourselves. The ancient adage "Know thyself" is a terrifying challenge from which we often flee.

Understanding ourselves as male and female persons is a lifelong endeavor. Each person has within himself or herself what can be thought of as masculine and feminine energy. The masculine seeks to reach out and create through differentiation in life; the feminine seeks to receive and hold life together in a harmonious whole.

Both the feminine and masculine principles are essential to living creatively. At times we must focus our attention and energy on a particular challenge, a special task. But eventually we must step back to try to understand how this task relates to the whole of our life and being. Sadly, men and women often fail to develop and draw upon both inner sources of creative energy. A man neglects his feminine qualities at the risk of becoming a pragmatist, giving technological answers to questions that demand human wisdom; a woman neglects her masculine qualities at the risk of being unable to exert leadership.

A blending or "inner marriage" of masculine and feminine qualities within each man and woman is essential today. When this blending happens, a man can seek to solve specific problems without losing sight of his relationship to life as a whole. A woman can contribute her vision of life as a whole and yet remain fully capable of individual, decisive actions.

Within the realm of self-knowledge, natural family planning takes on an added importance and dimension. Mary and Robert Joyce have written profoundly about the fully human power to generate new life, a power which originates in the depths of being.[4] We can think of the power to procreate human life solely in biological terms only if we view men and women simply as highly developed animals rather than as persons called to re-

---

[4] See, for example, Mary Rosera Joyce, *Love Responds to Life—The Challenge of Humanae Vitae* (Kenosha, Wis.: Prow, 1971), pp. 43–46.

spond to, and cooperate with, the God-life within them. Jesus said that the kingdom of God is within each one of us, and we seek to recognize and advance his kingdom by understanding and accepting our God-given human powers.

An essential facet of self-knowledge for any married couple, then, is an understanding of the procreative power which God has given to husband and wife. Today a couple can know when it is most possible for this power to reach fruition in new life. This knowledge was unavailable to our grandparents and only partially available, if at all, to our parents. A married couple today have the marvelous opportunity to live their entire conjugal life in awareness of their potential for procreating new life. As discussed in the previous chapter, the means for monitoring the fertile and infertile phases of a woman's menstrual cycle are readily available.

A married couple have two choices concerning the regulation of conception. First, they can use the knowledge provided by medical science to live in awareness of their procreative potential and with this awareness seek to conceive or to avoid the conception of new life. With this approach, husband and wife exercise a *stewardship* over the power of conception, receiving it as a gift from God over which they do not assume *absolute dominion or control*.[5] In natural family planning, a couple seek to understand and recognize their fertility, but they do not claim the right to alter or eliminate it, or assert that it is desirable or necessary to do so.

A second choice in family planning is to apply the technology of contraceptive devices and drugs to elimi-

---

[5] Francois and Michele Guy, *Tentative Twelve Principles of Natural Family Planning* (unpublished manuscript, 1973).

nate the fertile phase of the cycle or to prevent a viable conception (e.g., the abortifacient characteristics of some "pills" and the intrauterine device (IUD), which prevent the successful implantation and growth of a fertilized ovum). Through this choice, a husband and wife claim absolute dominion over their procreative powers by manipulating their fertility. The philosophical basis of this choice is at variance with that of natural family planning. A very reasonable question to ask is which of the two approaches offers the greater opportunity for increased self-knowledge and awareness and for growth in marital relationship.

We will deal only briefly here with the question of contraception, since it is outside the basic purview of this chapter. Certainly contraception affords little opportunity for greater self-knowledge and awareness, since its fundamental objective is to remove the dimension of fertility from the ongoing husband-wife dialogue. Some of the possible deeper consequences for the total relationship between husband and wife are reflected on by Mary Rosera Joyce.[6]

What are the potential problems of natural family planning? Few would question the value of a couple's mutual knowledge of the fertile and infertile phases of the wife's menstrual cycle. In fact, it seems self-evident that all women—married, single, or religious—should have the opportunity to live in awareness of their fertility variations. For example, we know several nuns who carefully observe their fertility changes and thus deepen their understanding of themselves as women and of what these changes mean in their relationship with God and the People of God, as celibate religious women.

---

[6] **Mary** Rosera Joyce, *The Meaning of Contraception*, (Collegeville, Minn.: The Liturgical Press, 1975).

Most objections to natural family planning center around the necessity for periodic continence. Certainly, in today's non-agricultural society most couples will not choose to have the very large families which characterized yesterday's rural America. The complexities and costs of rearing children today do not encourage having a large family. But what must be carefully ensured is that the decision to procreate is truly a voluntary one, reached within the stewardship of the couple and sheltered from overt external coercion. This will be a delicate task requiring much vigilance, given the real and imagined population concerns so vociferously expressed by governmental and non-governmental agencies alike.

Can periodic continence, freely chosen, be another avenue toward self-knowledge for husband and wife? We think it can be and is such an avenue. An understanding of the meaning of periodic continence, however, requires that we deepen our understanding of human sexuality and conjugal love. Without this depth of understanding, natural family planning becomes simply another contraceptive method. In the next chapter, we will begin to explore what periodic continence is *not* and what it can mean to the marriage relationship.

3

Periodic
Continence

It might be more logical and orderly to reflect first on the nature of human sexuality and the meaning of conjugal love before considering the subject of periodic continence. However, when natural family planning is discussed, continence is often cited as an objection to this approach. Furthermore, consideration of periodic continence can be a means for unlocking the mysteries of human sexuality and conjugal love.

Let us avoid any possible misunderstanding. Periodic continence refers to a married couple's choosing to express their love through coital sexual intercourse only during the infertile phases of the wife's menstrual cycle. This way of married life is often spoken of as "periodic abstinence," a terminology which gives us some important clues. Does it mean abstaining from "making love"? When periodic continence is thus defined, it indeed implies a very negative way of living—a turning on and off of expressions of affection by husband and wife.

But much more is possible with a true growth in conjugal love. Love within marriage can be expressed in many ways—verbally, emotionally, and physically. The expression of marital love in coital sexual intercourse is the unique and most dramatic way, but it is only one way. So often as the years pass there is danger of losing or neglecting the many and varied ways of showing love and concern that were present during the engagement period and the early years of marriage. Periodic continence helps us to show that we love our husband or wife at all times just because he or she *is*!

At this point we want to consider the term "sexual intercourse." It is commonly used to describe "that union of the genital organs of man and woman in which the penis is introduced into the vagina and deposits semen there."[7] John Marshall objects to this usage—with good reason, we think. He notes that a person's sexuality is what he or she is, not what he or she does. Hence, in a very real sense, all intercourse among people is sexual. Limiting the term "sexual intercourse" to genital union between a man and a woman is to fall into the error of equating sexuality with genital actions. It is both more precise and philosophically sound to describe the freely chosen genital union of a loving, committed husband and wife as coitus or coital sexual intercourse, and therefore we have used these terms rather than the more common one.

---

[7] John Marshall, *Catholics, Marriage and Contraception* (Baltimore: Helicon Press, 1965), pp. xi–xii.

We *are* our sexuality. This idea generates new potential to intensify the meaning of sexual intercourse. Any communication between two people is sexual and can be love-giving. Only the older woman in our society is allowed to express this kind of love, as society rightly considers that her actions have no coital implications. She can say to an unrelated male, "I love you," and have her meaning understood. True liberation will be achieved when men and women of all ages feel free to express love to each other in a celibate relationship.

Erich Fromm describes love as truly an art which can be mastered only with self-imposed discipline, intense concentration, and long patience.[8] The art of loving in marriage surely includes the myriad ways of showing love for each other, and unless we make a conscious effort to employ many of them, the relationship will suffer. Marriage is not a job to be worked at but a relationship to be intensely lived as consciously as possible. Periodic continence presents anew the opportunity to be in love each day, with emphasis on how this love is expressed in a constantly changing and dynamic manner.

It is sometimes said that periodic continence is an artificial repression of "sex" in marriage and thus is restrictive and harmful. This notion exhibits a very narrow view of human sexuality. On the contrary, periodic continence offers a true path toward sexual freedom. We are free only when we can *choose* to perform an action, without a sense of compulsion. The art of loving is not the instant gratification of felt needs. Coitus in marriage is not an automatic response to biological urges which our culture tells us must not be frustrated. As an expression of love in marriage, coital sexual intercourse has its

---

[8] Erich Fromm, *The Art of Loving* (New York: Bantam Edition, 1963), pp. 90–92.

deepest meaning when freely chosen by husband and wife, with full cognizance of their existing potential to conceive new life.

Years ago, when sexual matters were discussed one frequently would hear the terms "self-control" or "self-mastery." Today the featured term is "fulfillment." There is nothing wrong with any of these terms—they are merely incomplete. The idea associated with self-control or self-mastery is that we must not allow our biological drives to control our lives and actions, but must rather control or master them. The idea associated with fulfillment is that we must mature ourselves sexually, although too often this is narrowly limited to coital intercourse alone.

Robert and Mary Joyce note that the human person is called, not to dominate his sexuality, but to assimilate it, to receive it into the depths of his being.[9] All actions performed by a person are sexual, insofar as they reflect his masculinity or her femininity. Thus, true sexual fulfillment occurs when one receives one's sexuality into one's being and reflects this in all one does and says and all that one is. This person is truly "sexually active," even though he or she may be genitally uninvolved. For a person living his or her sexuality in this way, the question of self-mastery or sexual fulfillment is irrelevant.

Admittedly, the assimilation of our sexuality into the depths of our being is a lifelong challenge. Periodic continence practiced with natural family planning offers an opportunity to meet this challenge. Most human beings naturally shrink from the difficult, the apparent burden. Periodic continence confronts us with questions

---

[9] Mary Rosera Joyce and Robert E. Joyce, *New Dynamics in Sexual Love* (Collegeville, Minn.: St. John's University Press, 1970), p. 52.

about ourselves from which we cannot easily flee. To what extent is coital intercourse a deep expression of married love in our lives, and to what extent is it an impulsive response to urgently felt needs? Can we live a period of continence within a fully conjugal loving relationship? Honest answers to these questions say a great deal about the depth and maturity of conjugal love.

4

Dynamics of the
Marriage Relationship

Most couples begin marriage with high expectations for their life together. In many respects these expectations may not be realistic. They include, perhaps, a romantic concept that love will grow through the years, without recognition of the intensity, pain, and sensitivity to the other that will make this growth possible.

One thing is certain: the relationship between husband and wife which exists at the start of marriage will never again be the same. As both persons mature, develop new skills, and perceive the world differently, they are bound to relate to each other differently on their tenth, fifteenth, or twenty-fifth anniversary than during their first year of marriage. Either husband and wife will develop both individually and mutually, become more aware of each other and themselves, and achieve a deeper unity, or they will drift apart. The marriage relationship is never static; changes are inevitable, and those that occur will either build up or tear down the marriage. Either we will learn more about our beloved (and ourself) or we will soon know less, since the other person will have changed from what he or she was.

It is difficult to overemphasize that both husband and wife will change in many ways during the years after their wedding day. This process, of course, has always occurred, but the possibilities for change loom even greater today. The mobility of many Americans means that a family may live in many locations, often including diverse environments with cultural settings that stimulate the development of new interests. Moves will result in new friends, new social patterns, and new opportunities for educational and professional development.

Just as the outer environment is unlikely to remain static, so too the inner environment of the marriage is subject to change. In most marriages, the joy and responsibility of parenthood will significantly affect the thinking and attitudes of husband and wife. Each stage in the growth of a child brings new demands which require a sensitive and cooperative response from the child's mother and father. To cope with the ever-increasing demands that change brings both from within the marriage and from society, husband and wife need to draw upon a deepening mutual love for, and commitment to, each other.

What are some of the conditions through which change is accepted creatively, making a lifetime of growth in love between husband and wife possible? Three characteristics seem most important: an unreserved lifetime commitment to each other; fidelity to this commitment; and deep trust that the other person will also live up to it. To counterbalance the many changes that life brings, there is need for a stable point centered in the marriage commitment that husband and wife bring to each other without reservation or temporal limits. Love can grow and deepen when there is mutual trust, rock-like in its ability to weather any storm.

The case for trial marriage, temporary marriage, or limited-commitment marriage is often made on the grounds that mutual compatibility must be established or that a "sexual adjustment" must be tested. The irony of such "marriages" is that they contain within themselves a self-destructive mechanism of built-in obsolescence.

All marriages, involving as they do the most intimate relationship between a man and a woman, will undergo periods of stress which demand a creative response on the part of both parties. If the commitment to each other is made with reservations and conditions, such creative response is less likely. It is so much easier to say, "Well, we weren't sure this relationship would work out, and apparently it hasn't." Often patience and renewed efforts at communicating with and understanding the other will suggest the means of resolving the difficulties.

Florida Scott-Maxwell has written perceptively and poetically about men, women, and marriage. For most of recorded history, women have represented the private side of life, and men the public side. Women have been responsible for private relationships centered in a world of feeling and emotion. Men have been responsible for public relationships centered in a world of thought and action. Men have depended upon women to be the stable point, the holding center within marriage and the family.[10]

Many men may feel threatened by the need for assuming greater responsibility for the private sectors of life in marriage and the family. It is true that today many of the obvious stereotypes of sex roles have been discarded. Many husbands and fathers now willingly (or not so willingly) do chores in the kitchen, change diapers, take care of the children for periods of time, etc. This activity is all quite positive, but it is really only a beginning which, if not developed, will remain superficial.

What marriage and family life of the future require is a commitment in depth from both husband and wife. Consider two comments that a husband of the past (we hope) might have uttered: "She got pregnant again!" and "Why can't she keep those kids under control?" These statements reflect an immature sense of responsibility toward marriage and parenthood which has been characteristic of too many men. Natural family planning offers a real opportunity for a man to accept co-equal responsibility for bringing new life into the world. With the dynamic of periodic continence within the marital relationship, a husband can become more deeply sensitive to the varied expressions of conjugal love. The marriage relationship, he finds, cannot be taken for granted; it requires a sensitive, ongoing caring on the part of both husband and wife.

A man begins to place the private side of life in proper perspective when he realizes that he is first a husband and father, and secondly a butcher, banker, or candlestick-maker. When there are genuine conflicts be-

---

[10] Florida Scott-Maxwell, *Women and Sometimes Men* (New York: Harper & Row, 1971), pp. 11–13.

tween professional demands and family responsibilities, it should be clear where priorities lie. It is only too obvious that marriages today are failing to survive the stress of ill-placed priorities.

Women are now rightfully demanding a place in the public sector of life. A woman's acceptance does not require a professional status but, rather, widespread recognition of her as person, apart from any relationship she has as wife and mother. This is not to say that her relationships are downgraded; rather, they are enhanced when she approaches them with a greater sense of personal self-worth.

A balance is maintained if men begin to assume a greater responsibility for private relationships and develop a heightened sensitivity to what they must contribute to them. It is not unreasonable to suggest that natural family planning can help toward this goal.

Women's historic "role" of holding a society together by assuming most of the responsibility for private relationships is now changing. *Heritage*, "herstory," has been largely oral tradition, extremely important but rarely written down, since the details of marriage and family life were so similar all over the world. Only if woman entered the masculine world of *history* were her activities noted, mainly because of their uniqueness.

The masculine quality to thrust (power) and the feminine quality to hold (wisdom) complement each other. As women publicly express their thrusting power, men as a group are challenged to attain the wisdom to hold that power. This role is new and awkward for men, just as the public power thrust is for women.

The diverse ethnic expressions of faith and important family events within marriage were cultivated by women and handed down by example to the next generation. Woman's complement to the *his*tory of man is *her*itage. In an age when women are thrusting into history, it is imperative that men become accustomed to transmitting heritage. If history and heritage, power and wisdom, are not in balance, chaos results.

When husband and wife together assume the responsibility for living in awareness of their procreative potential, they are sharing the most fundamental marital decision involving power and wisdom—the procreation of new life in cooperation with God. They can assume mutual responsibility for guiding their children through their developing years with a deepening awareness of the richness of a family's history and heritage. Not least, they can assume responsibility for bringing forth the God-life in each other.

5

Communication

The vital importance of communication in marriage has always been recognized and in our lifetime has received almost endless attention. The ability to express our thoughts, feelings, and attitudes to another person in a comprehensible way is essential if we are really to get to know one another. Obviously, if communication is to take place, each person must be able to communicate. In a sense, communication is like a magnetic field which each person creates, drawing the other to him or her and being drawn to the other. The strength of this force of giving and receiving determines whether they both become "locked in" because of the strong force of one or both, or whether each tends to "spin off" because of "weak attraction." The giving and receiving must respect the ecological balance so that each person remains free for independent action but attracted enough to maintain and deepen the relationship. This magnetic force flows not only between individuals but also between groups of persons. Authentic communication between different peoples of the world, both on a governmental level and on a person-to-person basis, is no longer an optional extra in our post-Manhattan Project age.

At one level, communication is verbal, that is, imparting the oral or written word. Even at this level, problems can block or contracept a potential dialogue, a creating of a magnetic field. We are all too familiar with the scene of two people arguing or talking rapidly and loudly at each other, neither hearing a word spoken by the other. Sounds are rushing through the air in a seemingly endless torrent, but no real communication is taking place, for the receiver is not attuned. What is missing is the essential ingredient of listening carefully to what the other person is saying. Communication implies not only the exposition of one's own views but also the willingness to listen to and react to another's viewpoint.

The importance of communication is apparent in the many innovative techniques that have been tried in recent years. Group sensitivity and group therapy sessions have explored different styles of communication, both verbal and non-verbal. The popularity of Marriage Encounter certainly shows the need people feel for improving their ability to communicate within marriage. The technique of a husband and wife writing to each other on common matters of feeling and concern, and then examining what has been written, is apparently a device effective in breaking down barriers restricting oral communication.

Communication involves more than the written and spoken word. We communicate by our posture, our tone of voice, our facial expressions, the implied attitudes and values behind what we say, and even, or perhaps especially, by our silence. It is a truism that we teach our children much more by what we are and do than by what we say. For example, the way in which a man and a woman live their marriage, their ability or inability to express affection to each other in ordinary ways and situations, says much more to their children about marriage than any words can. When parents seek to explain to their youngsters the bodily changes that will occur in their growth to manhood and womanhood, the words they choose are certainly important; but the attitudes and values associated with the words convey much to the son or daughter concerning how a parent feels about his or her sexuality.

Communication takes place on various levels in marriage. Periodic continence challenges the ability of a couple to communicate their love, caring, and respect for each other in many ways. All expressions of love occur through sexual intercourse. However, when love is expressed mainly or solely by coital union, the conjugal relationship becomes one-dimensional. This perspective gives a distorted view of the marital relationship. The many ways of expressing love reinforce the meaning of coital union. A caressing touch, a tender glance, a thoughtful gift, a private joke, an anticipated need—all are good in themselves and enhance coitus as a deep expression of conjugal love. Through periodic continence, a couple are challenged to explore many different ways of communicating their love to each other. Admittedly, this dimension in marriage can occur without periodic continence. However, the experiences of many couples

suggest an intensification of communication at all levels
of marriage when periodic continence is accepted as a
positive value within the total relationship between husband and wife.

Good communication is an art which must be developed in every marriage, but it is not a goal in itself.
It is really a development toward communion—a heightened unity in marriage. Mary and Robert Joyce note
that communication has its own inherent limitations:
"Friends, ... are persons who can mutually actualize
the potencies of each other by communicating what they
have in their being's possession. We are able to communicate the things that we have, but we are unable to communicate the being that we are."[11] We treasure those
moments in life when our being is in communion with
another person. Communication is not necessary then.
In fact, there is nothing to be said!

Alan Watts describes happiness as existing in the
ancient advice, "Become what you are." He speaks of
self-abandonment to life and of the dance of life. Happiness cannot be striven for but consists in living life
from moment to moment, accepting one's own being in
the awareness that nothing is unrelated to it.[12]

Communion with another person—one being touch-
ing another being—cannot be attained through sheer
effort. It comes with acceptance—acceptance of our own
being and acceptance of the whole person whom we love.
We accept others when we are aware of, and rejoice in,
all their creative potential. Natural family planning can
provide one small but fundamental support for the communion of persons in marriage.

[11] *New Dynamics in Sexual Love*, p. 28.
[12] Alan W. Watts, *The Meaning of Happiness* (New York:
Harper & Row, 1970), pp. 186–187.

6

Conjugal Love and
Human Sexuality

It is hard to think of another word in the English language that is used and abused as frequently as the word "love." In answer to misguided appeals to "love of country," terrible carnages have been visited on other peoples. In romantic lore we "make love," "fall in love," and with surprising alacrity "fall out of love."

Love, in its deepest meaning, signifies the total, unreserved giving of oneself and the total, unreserved receiving of the loved one. This unreserved giving includes even one's life. Jesus, who came to give life in greater abundance, said: "The greatest love a man can have for his friends is to give his life for them" (John 15:13), and: "A new commandment I give you: love one another. As

I have loved you, so you must love one another" (John 13:34). Most of us blush at the command, "Love your enemies" (Luke 6:27). The Christian ideal of love has touched the hearts of individuals who have truly become candles to light the darkness. One thinks immediately of the heroic work of Mother Teresa in India, Dorothy Day in New York, Viktor Frankl in Germany, and Albert Schweitzer in Africa. Love has inspired some of the noblest human lives and some of the most exalted deeds. It has also been invoked in many of the sorriest human episodes.

What are some of the signs or characteristics of love? Erich Fromm speaks of four elements common to all of its forms: care, responsibility, respect, and knowledge. He defines love as the "active concern for the life and the growth of that which we love."[13] This is genuine caring. We are ready at the same time to assume responsibility for the loved one and to be responsible in our mutual relationship. We respect those whom we love, not only for what they are but for what they can be—for all their potential. Our love impels us to the endless and inexhaustible quest of knowing the person loved.

Can two people—a man and a woman—live and love intensely without entering into a coital relationship? The answer to this question indicates a direction into the future of hope or hopelessness. If we can affirm that it is possible for a man and a woman to live and love—physically, emotionally, and spiritually—without entering into a coital relationship, we may be on the brink of a new Eden to redeem the chaos of the first. Perhaps we are finally becoming aware of a powerful idea whose time has come. We may be entering a new epoch and, to para-

---

[13] *The Art of Loving*, p. 22.

phrase T. de Chardin, mastering the meaning of love and discovering fire for the second time. Although this may be pathologically optimistic, perhaps we are capable of "blasting off" into the space-time mystery of the man-woman relationship.

For a variety of reasons—mechanized technology for one—many Western peoples seem to have developed a non-contact way of living. Each man and woman is an island. Any tactile expression of affection is immediately suspect of seductive intention. In fact, such people, upon tactile contact with another, may be so astonished that they actually precipitate the kindling of strong feelings. In reaction, they initiate an even stronger hands-off policy, spinning with each generation harder and ever harder shells of self-protection.

The antidote to this disease of loneliness is to take the honest risk of cracking out of our shells to make contact with persons with whom we are building a sense of trust. The risk, though real, is minimized if the group or community of people one associates with understands the principles on which one bases the freedom of these actions. The fundamental principle is to live responsibly—true to one's commitments and respectful of the commitments of others in the group. In this environment a hug, a kiss, an embrace, a long conversation, or a confidence is understood to be what it is—an expression of caring. A husband does not become suspicious of his wife's caring for another man and her expression of this. He knows of her conjugal commitment to him and has experienced trust in her. His trust of his fellow man is also strong, for he knows full well that each respects him and accepts the principles of a celibate love relationship. He understands his wife's relationship because he, too, experiences the same type of relationship with other women. Husband and wife know that these relationships have freed them into a whole new world of love for others while intensifying their love for each other.

Of the many crises of energy in this world, not the least is the waste of human sexual energy. Sexual energy, respectfully and responsibly expressed, could warm the environment of human relationship and put an end to frigidity. Coital conjugal love cannot exist in a vacuum, to be turned on and off. Love must be given and received among many people (friends). Otherwise, no matter how hot the conjugal fire is, it is destined to cool. If, however, as conjugal lovers go about their daily lives, sometimes together, sometimes apart, and experience the warmth of human contact with others, each grows in love of self and love of the other. This love experienced by each of them brings warmth and intensity to their own monogamous relationship, which in turn sends them forth with vigor to encounter all whom they love.

Conjugal love, unlike celibate love, is unique in its exclusiveness and possible fruition in new life. The love that husband and wife experience in each other will profoundly affect their capacity for parental love of their children and for their love for fellow human beings. However, like all expressions of love, the reality of conjugal love can be seen in the degree of caring, responsibility, respect, and knowledge that is present.[14]

There is much to reflect upon concerning the value that natural family planning can have in the growth of conjugal love. As we noted in Chapter 1, fertility awareness includes knowing the procreative potential of a particular coital expression of love. To be aware of this procreative dimension and consciously call forth God's

---

[14] *The Art of Loving,* p. 22.

cooperation in a loving relationship is to participate fully in procreation. Refraining from coital expressions of love during the peak of procreative potential is a renewed witness of both husband and wife of their respect for this potential. Together they share the knowledge of their fertility and together assume responsibility for expressing their love in the light of this knowledge.

Periodic continence during the fertile time, rather than stifling expressions of love, challenges a couple to increase their "response-ability" toward each other. Living this way of married life enables a couple to break through the utilitarian "love-machine," "baby-machine," compartmentalized view of human sexuality. Imbued with the serenity of a dynamic unity in love, a couple's relationship is totally fertile, creative, and loving. Coitus is experienced as an openness to the life of each other, with all of its potential.

We are plagued today with the problem of the unwanted pregnancy, often extrapolated to include the "unwanted child." The wanted/unwanted syndrome grows naturally out of a society steeped in an ethic of consumerism. When increasing levels of consumption are constantly stimulated and planned, there is little room for the unexpected and little tolerance of it. We want to follow the "game plan" and refuse to tolerate deviations from it.

When men and women demand absolute technological dominion over the power to procreate new life, the unexpected pregnancy may be very difficult to accept. But when the procreative power is received in stewardship by husband and wife, other attitudes are possible. Coitus is always viewed as an expression of love which contains within it the potential for activating the procreative power given to husband and wife. Procreation as the result of a particular coital expression of love may be thought of as extremely improbable, but never impossible. It is meritorious and valid to strive for a high degree of reliability in predicting the fertile and infertile phases of the menstrual cycle, but accurate prediction is far from the ultimate goal in marriage. When a couple are stewards of their procreative power, conception of new life is never unthinkable, however unlikely it may be. This dimension in living a conjugal life eliminates the utilitarian concept of the wanted and unwanted child which is undermining family life today.

It has been suggested that natural family planning, because it removes the spontaneity and freedom from expressions of married love, is not really "natural" at all. Paradoxically, such a viewpoint reflects a static concept of married love and a one-dimensional view of its expression in coital sexual intercourse. If the expression of love in marriage is an art, it must be dynamic and multifaceted. There is a spontaneity in the expression of married love, but it is a refined spontaneity. There is all the difference in the world between the spontaneity of a skilled pianist performing a musical masterpiece and the spontaneity of a three-year-old child banging away at the piano.

It is paradoxical that when love is not expressed coitally for a time, out of respect for a couple's procreative power, its renewed expressions are that much more spontaneous and meaningful. A bouquet of roses is admittedly beautiful. But the beauty of the rose is only enhanced when interspersed with other types of flowers. A diamond is all the more resplendent within a setting of other precious stones. The unique beauty and meaning of coital love in marriage are all the more evident if husband and wife, for a time, place special emphasis on showing love to each other in other ways. While the analogy is not perfect, consider for a moment the chrysanthemum. If it receives no care, the plant grows too tall and spindly to support the weight of even small flowers. However, if during the summer season the new growth is periodically clipped, the plant will develop fuller foliage, deeper roots, a stronger stem, and more abundant flowers. So, too, coital expressions of love have their deepest meaning and bloom all the more resplendent when cultivated within a setting of conjugal love expressed in many ways.

7

Developing Respect for
Fertility in the Family

The term "sex education" arouses deep emotional feelings in many people. The question of explicitly focusing upon sexual development in public education has been and continues to be a controversial issue. Regardless of where one stands on this question, it must be recognized that parents are the primary educators of their children in the very basic process of helping them to become aware of the meaning of their sexuality.

Today we constantly hear about all the potential "hang-ups" that can exist between parents and children, blocking effective communication and stifling an honest, open relationship. Natural family planning seen in the dimension of fertility awareness can be a great aid in removing this deficiency. When husband and wife are at ease with each other in an ongoing dialogue concerning their sexuality and procreative power, communication with their children flows more freely.

The unfolding of the meaning of sexuality is a very gradual process for a child. Parents are uniquely able to guide and challenge a child in his or her personal development. Rather than tortuous discussions about "the birds and the bees," a child slowly becomes aware of the values which parents share and express regarding their sexuality. Obviously, this communication between parents and child respects the stage of the child's development. The family does not one day sit down and "talk about sex." Rather, parents, through an ongoing dialogue with their children, share their values by living them. If parents have been living in a love relationship such as we have spoken of earlier, their own dialogue and ease of communicating with each other are reflected in their relationships with the sexual persons who are their children.

A mother and father can help their children to understand the meaning of the menstrual cycle, as well as review with them the proper vocabulary used to describe this process. Just as the seasons of the year give signs of their approach and presence, so too the "seasons" of the menstrual cycle give "signs" of their approach and presence. Children may be helped to view this pattern as the "inner environment" of women, with as much intricacy in its ecology as the outer environment of land, air, and water.

The cycle of life may be viewed as beginning in autumn. At this time the trees in all their rich, vibrant color drop their leaves and begin again to prepare for new growth. So, too, the uterus sloughs off its lining as an ovum (egg) begins its early preparation toward maturity. The sign of this "season" is menstruation.

Autumn slowly gives way to winter. During winter there is a cooling of the atmosphere, and the earth appears barren, even though imperceptible growth is occurring. The signs of a woman's "winter" are a slight cooling of her body temperature while she is at rest and a sensation of vaginal dryness. The number of days of her "winter" will vary, depending upon the length of time it takes for a particular ovum to reach maturity. This determines the length of the entire cycle. Some women and girls have long "winters," creating long cycles, while others have short "winters," creating short cycles.

Winter is eventually succeeded by spring. Spring is a time when there is a bursting forth, a flowering, and a fragrance that is unique to this season. During a woman's "springtime," the ovum prepares to erupt and then bursts forth from an ovary. It is strongly attracted toward the Fallopian tube, which it enters. The life of the ovum is measured in hours. The "springtime" of each cycle is a reminder to a woman of her potential to conceive and nurture a new human being. There are two signs of "spring." The first sign is a developing emission of a healthy, crystal-clear vaginal discharge. This discharge may be cloudy at first, but it gradually becomes clear and then begins to disappear. This process occurs over many days. The second sign of "spring" is the shift of a woman's body temperature to a slightly higher level after ovulation.

Spring moves into the season of summer, a time characterized by warmth and continuing lushness. The "summer" of a woman's cycle lasts about two weeks, during which time the lining of the uterus continues to grow. The signs of "summer" are a sensation of vaginal dryness and a continuing higher level of body temperature.

As a young girl learns about her menstrual cycle, she awakens to the realization that she is the personification of a "springtime" long ago. Her conception lent a new dimension to the following "summer," which lasted for the duration of her prenatal life. These realizations give her the opportunity to sense in a wholesome way the potential of her own "springtime" and help her to develop a profound reverence for her dignity as a person. In her relationships she can then summon all the strength within her to require others to respect her as she is. It seems that nothing less than this intense respect for her own dignity will suffice in the age in which we live.

A young man can also develop an appreciation of his sexuality as he comes to understand how new life begins. When he becomes aware of his own power to procreate new life, as well as of the intricacy of the menstrual cycle, he can gain a profound appreciation of the potential of coital union. Through his parents' witness, he comes to realize that the power within him calls for genuine responsibility in his personal relationships.

Our hope for the future is that each young woman may learn to accept and to live with the "seasons" of her cycle. If she enters into a conjugal commitment, this hope can only be fulfilled if she marries "a man for all seasons."

8

Marriage as Sacrament

Most of the thoughts expressed in previous chapters concerning the potential value of natural family planning in marriage do not presuppose any value system or point of view other than that of two people living their marriage within a permanent monogamous commitment and seeking to enrich their conjugal love. Many men and women without any specific faith-commitment or supernatural orientation could be drawn toward this way of married life. However, those couples within the Judeo-Christian faith can search for an even deeper meaning. The deeper meaning for Catholics comes from their belief that marriage is one of the seven sacraments instituted by Jesus.

Saint Paul, in his First Letter to the Corinthians, tells us: "Christ is like a single body, which has many parts; it is still one body, even though it is made up of different parts" (12:12). Later, in the same chapter, he says: "If one part of the body suffers, all the other parts suffer with it; if one part is praised, all other parts share its happiness. All of you, then, are Christ's body and each one is a part of it" (12:26-27). Thus, through the sacrament of baptism, all Christians share in the life of Jesus, and through him bear a special relationship and responsibility to each other. We are indeed our brother's keeper, especially our brothers and sisters in the faith.

This fundamental unity in Christ which all Christians possess is re-celebrated and deepened when a man and a woman are united in the sacrament of matrimony. The dignity of marriage and the radical meaning of married love are clearly brought out by Saint Paul in his Letter to the Ephesians when he exhorts: "Husbands, love your wives in the same way that Christ loved the Church and gave his life for it" (5:25). And later in the same place: "Men ought to love their wives just as they love their own bodies. A man who loves his wife loves himself. No one ever hates his own body. Instead, he feeds it and takes care of it, just as Christ does the Church, for we are members of his body" (5:28-30). In sacramental marriage, husband and wife are called to love each other with the commitment and depth that Jesus shows for his Church.

This is a great mystery and a majestic calling in Christian life. In a special way husband and wife, through their creative and fruitful love for each other, are called to help each other directly realize his or her Christian potential. Through a creative and fruitful love, each encounters Jesus in the other. With a creative and fruitful love, husband and wife respond to the God-life in each other and together reach out to all members of the Church, the Body of Christ.

The meaning of natural family planning can deepen within the sacramental relationship of marriage. Fertility awareness is an openness to all the fertile God-life that husband and wife experience in each other. Our actions within an interpersonal relationship are fertile when we freely respond to the grace God gives to us and the other person. This response requires a great sensitivity to the other person as well as a deep awareness of his or her creative potential. Sensitivity and awareness proceed not so much from great individual effort as from a willingness to receive and respond to the gift of grace, i.e., God-life, given in marriage.

The procreative dimension of fertility awareness becomes a sacred trust in sacramental marriage. Husband and wife assume a stewardship of the power to bring new life into the world, that is, new members of the Body of Christ. It is indeed a sacred trust to call forth into the future our spiritual heritage, to participate in the growth of God's kingdom. When we come to realize that our procreative power is a gift, a sacred trust from God, then we see in a new light the opportunity to live in greater awareness of this power. Conscious parenthood becomes, not an optional extra, but a way of most fully living our Catholic faith in sacramental marriage.

9

Marriage and Community:
The Future

We live in a very exciting time of rapid and ever accelerating change. Perhaps it is human nature always to feel that the years gone by were more stable and that the time we live in now is totally different and unique. The developments of technology derived from rapidly increasing knowledge in the physical, chemical, and life sciences are undeniably unique to our age. The rapidity with which new knowledge is translated into technology affecting our daily lives is also unique. Certainly, however, not all the questions which arise from the possible use of technology are entirely novel to human experience. The fundamental need remains the same—acquiring the wisdom to use the technology for the material and spiritual betterment of all mankind. It is never enough just to ask the question, "Can we do it?" We may not do all that we can do. We must first seek to understand the meaning of what we do, not in terms of a single problem, but in relation to all of life.

What does the future hold for marriage and family life? Many prophets of gloom and doom question whether the family and marriage as we have known them have any real future. Alternative lifestyles are proposed with enthusiasm: "communities" of singles; group "marriage"; sequential "marriages," responsive to the changing needs of a person throughout his or her lifetime, etc. Proponents of new lifestyles point to the staggering divorce rates as evidence that permanent monogamous marriages are not working. They say that in an age of enlightened sexuality it is unrealistic to expect or demand of people a way of life in accordance with the moral teachings of the Judeo-Christian tradition.

Marriage and family life are under pressure from yet another group—the population-explosion people, whose major axiom is that the future of the world is threatened by uncontrolled population growth and that the first order of business is to stop it at almost any cost. The methods proposed include contraception, sterilization, abortion, and euthanasia. In their single-minded devotion to the cause of zero or negative population growth, they ignore or minimize other considerations: (a) the rapidly declining birth rates among the developed nations; (b) the population implosion, which concentrates people into limited urban areas (crowding into cities is as old as civilization); (c) the natural decline in birth rates which occurs when a country emerges from an undeveloped to a developed status; (d) the ever more effective use of the earth's resources to provide food and other basic needs for man; and (e) the misuse of the earth's resources to the detriment of our environment (one hundred million cars for some two hundred million people in the United States is but an example). Volumes have been written on the population question, but the point to be made is that pressures stemming from concern about it strongly impact on the future of the family.

What are we to make of all this, and what does it have to do with natural family planning? We see the importance of natural family planning revealed in two ways. First, it leads to a fundamental reverence for life which rejects the substitution of pragmatism for human wisdom in solving life's problems. Secondly, it provides an alternative to contraception in marriage.

Let us deal briefly with the question of contraception. Here we must choose our words very carefully; nothing to be said is intended to impugn the motives or sincerity of married couples who are practicing contraception. In the first place, few of these couples ever felt they had any real alternative.

However, having said this, a suspicion remains that a society in which the practice of contraception is generally accepted and approved will tend to become a society which will accept technological solutions to problems posed by life after conception. We air this suspicion with full realization that there is a world of difference between contraception and abortion, for example. A true contraceptive (and this excludes probable abortifacients such as the IUD and many pills) prevents the conception of new life. Abortion, in contrast, terminates new human life after conception. Abortion and contraception are very different, it is true, but if we listen to what is being said, we must reflect further.

Abortion is widely proposed as the "fail-safe" birth control method, the solution to contraceptive "failures."

Of course, many married couples practicing contraception would never consider abortion. But when contraception is proposed as an absolute solution to the "problem" of family planning and its technology fails, society and individuals tend to seek another technological solution to the "unwanted pregnancy." When the human power to procreate new life is eliminated or tampered with through contraceptive technology, the attitudinal reorientation may lead to technological manipulation of life itself.

Natural family planning can help to provide a totally different attitude toward life. It fosters the ability to see the procreative power as a gift from God which husband and wife gratefully accept and minister to each other. Rather than a problem to be eliminated in whatever way possible, fertility is seen as a potential to be known and respected. Respect for fertility is related to an all-encompassing reverence for life and an appreciation of the totality of God's creation. If the very power to procreate new life is respected and the responsibility for ministering this power accepted, then new life, which is the incarnation of this power, will be all the more revered.

Monogamous marriage as a lifetime commitment within Judeo-Christian tradition is under attack in our modern world. It is rejected by many who never really delve deeply into the meaning of such a commitment. The question of birth regulation within the Catholic tradition is treated in the same way.

Specifically, within the Catholic faith, the old, rather simple ways of dividing marriage into primary and secondary purposes and heavily emphasizing the procreative purpose of coital sexual intercourse have been found wanting. Greater insight is developing into the relationship between husband and wife in terms of their mutual love and commitment. But an evolving understanding of the meaning of coital sexual intercourse in marriage does not rightly include a denial of its procreative dimension.

If monogamous marriage is to endure, we must answer the challenge of greatly deepening our understanding of the marital commitment. Natural family planning can provide an impetus toward answering this challenge. The couple-to-couple approach to teaching natural family planning can be a beginning point for this journey.

This will be a journey into the future, not a foray into the past to recapture a so-called golden age of family stability. Too often in the recent past, stable family life (i.e., no divorce or separation) was achieved only on the level of a commandment or justice. When love was absent or destroyed, the gospel prohibition of divorce by Jesus was accepted literally and absolutely. Or, when love failed, husband and wife regarded continuing the marriage as a just obligation to spouse or children. Society tended to support the objective of keeping a marriage going, both through its laws, which made a divorce difficult to obtain, and through its prevailing attitudes toward divorce.

Clearly, this situation has changed greatly in the past twenty or thirty years. Divorce is ever more commonly acceptable and obtainable. Living on a commandment or justice level in marriage is increasingly repugnant in an age when "personal fulfillment" is a new god. Even among Catholics, there is questioning of the absoluteness of the gospel prohibition of divorce. It seems clear that permanent monogamous marriages of the future will flounder if lived on a commandment or justice level alone. Future shock demands a new intensity in conjugal life, a deeper understanding of conjugal love, and a willingness to search for and discover anew the meaning of personal, perpetual commitment in love.

A quest of a lifetime, a probing for the meaning of the most important human commitment that most people make is not easily done in isolation. The couple-to-couple approach of teaching natural family planning must grow to a couple-to-couple sharing and probing of the mystery of marriage. These searchings take on their fullest meaning when they are enlightened by a common faith and heritage. Never has there been a greater need for communities of Christian couples to search and learn together. To become fully what we are called to be in Christ, we must know what we are. Fertility awareness, in all its dimensions, is essential to this process.

Bibliography

Natural Family Planning

Billings, John J. *Natural Family Planning—The Ovulation Method.* Collegeville, Minn.: The Liturgical Press, third American edition, 1975.

Kippley, John and Sheila. *The Art of Natural Family Planning.* Cincinnati, Ohio: The Couple to Couple League International, 1975. Also available from The Liturgical Press, Collegeville, Minn.

Planning Your Family the S-T Way. Ottawa: SERENA of Canada, 1976. Available from The Liturgical Press, Collegeville, Minn.

Thyma, Paul. *The Double Check Method of Natural Family Planning.* Fall River, Mass.: Married Life Information Service, 1976.

Marriage, Personhood, and Human Sexuality

Fromm, Erich. *The Art of Loving.* New York: Bantam Books, Inc., 1963.

Joyce, Mary Rosera. *The Meaning of Contraception.* Collegeville, Minn.: The Liturgical Press, 1975.

————. *Love Responds to Life—The Challenge of Humanae Vitae.* Kenosha, Wis.: Prow, 1971.

———— and Robert E. Joyce. *New Dynamics in Sexual Love.* Collegeville, Minn.: St. John's University Press, 1970.

Kippley, John. *Birth Control and the Marriage Covenant.* Collegeville, Minn.: The Liturgical Press, 1976.

Scott-Maxwell, Florida. *Women and Sometimes Men.* New York: Perennial Library, Harper & Row, 1971.

Watts, Alan W. *The Meaning of Happiness.* New York: Perennial Library, Harper & Row, 1970.